Jane Addams

A Function of the Social Settlement

Jane Addams

A Function of the Social Settlement

ISBN/EAN: 9783337606411

Printed in Europe, USA, Canada, Australia, Japan

Cover: Foto ©Suzi / pixelio.de

More available books at **www.hansebooks.com**

PUBLICATIONS OF

THE AMERICAN ACADEMY OP POLITICAL AND SOCIAL SCIENCE

No. 251.

Issued Fortnightly.   May 16, 1899

A Function of the Social Settlement.

BY

Miss JANE ADDAMS,
Hull House, Chicago, Ill.

*A PAPER SUBMITTED TO THE AMERICAN ACADEMY OF POLITICAL
AND SOCIAL SCIENCE*

PHILADELPHIA
AMERICAN ACADEMY OF POLITICAL AND
SOCIAL SCIENCE.
moulin digital editions

2018

A FUNCTION OF THE SOCIAL SETTLEMENT.

The word "settlement," which we have borrowed from London, is apt to grate a little upon American ears. It is not, after all, so long ago that Americans who settled were those who had adventured into a new country, where they were pioneers in the midst of difficult surroundings. The word still implies migrating from one condition of life to another totally unlike it, and against this implication the resident of an American settlement takes alarm.

We do not like to acknowledge that Americans are divided into "two nations," as her prime minister once admitted of England. We are not willing, openly and professedly, to assume that American citizens are broken up into classes, even if we make that assumption the preface to a plea that the superior class has duties to the inferior. Our democracy is still our most precious possession, and we do well to resent any inroads upon it, even although they may be made in the name of philanthropy.

And yet because of this very democracy, superior privileges carry with them a certain sense of embarrassment, founded on the suspicion that intellectual and moral superiority too often rest upon economic props which are, after all, matters of accident, and that for an increasing number of young people the only possible way to be comfortable in the possession of those privileges, which result from educational advantages, is in an effort to make common that which was special and aristocratic. Added to this altruistic compunction one may easily discover a selfish suspicion that advantages thus held apart slowly crumble in their napkins, and are not worth having.

The American settlement, perhaps, has represented not so much a sense of duty of the privileged toward the unprivileged, of the "haves" to the "have nots," to borrow Canon Barnett's phrase, as a desire to equalize through social effort those results which superior opportunity may have given the possessor.

The settlement, however, certainly represents more than compunctions. Otherwise it would be but "the monastery of the nineteenth century," as it is indeed sometimes called, substituting the anodyne of work for that of contemplation, but still the old attempt to seek individual escape from the common misery through the solace of healing.

If this were the basis of the settlement, there would no longer be need of it when society had become reconstructed to the point of affording equal opportunity for all, and it would still be at the bottom a philanthropy, although expressed in social and democratic terms. There is, however, a sterner and more enduring aspect of the settlement which this paper would attempt to present.

It is frequently stated that the most pressing problem of modern life is that of a reconstruction and a reorganization of the knowledge which we possess; that we are at last struggling to realize in terms of life all that has been discovered and absorbed, to make it over into healthy and direct expressions of free living. Dr. John Dewey, of the University of Chicago, has written: "Knowledge is no longer its own justification, the interest in it has at last transferred itself from accumulation and verification to its application to life." And he adds: "When a theory of knowledge forgets that its value rests in solving the problem out of which it has arisen, that of securing a method of action, knowledge begins to cumber the ground. It is a luxury, and becomes a social nuisance and disturber."

We may quote further from Professor James, of Harvard University, who recently said in an address before the Philosophical Union of the University of California: "Beliefs, in short, are really rules of action, and the whole function of thinking is but one step in the production of habits of action," or "the ultimate test for us of what a truth means is indeed the conduct it dictates or inspires."

Having thus the support of two philosophers, let us assume that the dominating interest in knowledge has become its use, the conditions under which, and ways in which it may be most effectively employed in human conduct; and that at last certain people have consciously formed themselves into groups for the express purpose of effective application. These groups which are called settlements have naturally sought the spots where the dearth of this applied knowledge was most obvious, the depressed quarters of great cities. They gravitate to these spots, not with the object of finding clinical material, not to found "sociological laboratories," not, indeed, with the analytical motive at all, but rather in a reaction from that motive, with a desire to use synthetically and directly whatever knowledge they, as a group, may possess, to test its validity and to discover the conditions under which this knowledge may be employed.

That, just as groups of men, for hundreds of years, have organized themselves into colleges, for the purpose of handing on and disseminating knowledge already accumulated, and as other groups have been organized into seminars and universities, for the purpose of research and the extension of the bounds of knowledge, so at last groups have been consciously formed for the purpose of the application of knowledge to life. This third attempt also would claim for itself the enthusiasm and advantage of collective living. It has come to be a group of people who share their methods, and who mean to make experience continuous beyond the individual. It may be urged that this function of application has always been undertaken by individuals and unconscious groups. This is doubtless true, just as much classic learning has always been disseminated outside of the colleges, and just as some of the most notable discoveries of pure science have been made outside of the universities. Still both these institutions do in the main accomplish the bulk of the disseminating, and the discovering; and it is upon the same basis that the third group may establish its value.

A FUNCTION OF THE SOCIAL SETTLEMENT

The ideal and developed settlement would attempt to test the value of human knowledge by action, and realization, quite as the complete and ideal university would concern itself with the discovery of knowledge in all branches. The settlement stands for application as opposed to research; for emotion as opposed to abstraction, for universal interest as opposed to specialization. This certainly claims too much, absurdly too much, for a settlement, in the light of its achievements, but perhaps not in the light of its possibilities.

This, then, will be my definition of the settlement: that it is an attempt to express the meaning of life in terms of life itself, in forms of activity. There is no doubt that the deed often reveals when the idea does not, just as art makes us understand and feel what might be incomprehensible and inexpressible in the form of an argument. And as the artist tests the success of his art when the recipient feels that he knew the thing before, but had not been able to express it, so the settlement, when it attempts to reveal and apply knowledge, deems its results practicable, when it has made knowledge available which before was abstract, when through use, it has made common that knowledge which was partial before, because it could only be apprehended by the intellect.

The chief characteristic of art lies in freeing the individual from a sense of separation and isolation in his emotional experience, and has usually been accomplished through painting, writing and singing; but this does not make it in the least impossible that it is now being tried, self-consciously and most bunglingly we will all admit, in terms of life itself.

A settlement brings to its aid all possible methods to reveal and make common its conception of life. All those arts and devices which express kindly relation from man to man, from charitable effort to the most specialized social intercourse, are constantly tried. There is the historic statement, the literary presentation, the fellowship which comes when great questions are studied with the hope of modifying actual conditions, the putting forward of the essential that the trivial may appear unimportant, as it is, the attempt to select the more typical and enduring forms of social life, and to eliminate, as far as possible, the irrelevant things which crowd into actual living. There are so-called art exhibits, concerts, dramatic representations, every possible device to make operative on the life around it, the conception of life which the settlement group holds. The demonstration is made not by reason, but by life itself. There must, of course, be a certain talent for conduct and unremitting care lest there grow to be a divergence between theory and living, for however embarrassing this divergence may prove in other situations, in a settlement the artist throws away his tools as soon as this thing happens. He is constantly transmitting by means of his human activity, his notion of life to others. He hopes to produce a sense of infection which may ultimately result in identity of interest.

Merely to produce a sense of infection would be art, but to carry with it a consciousness of participation and responsibility would be the moralizing and application of art. We may illustrate this with that form of art which is most general and prevalent among us, the art of novel writing. No one who has ever read Zangwill's "Children of the Ghetto" can afterwards walk through the Jewish quarter of any great city without a quickening of the blood as he passes. He must feel a momentary touch of the poetry and fidelity which are fostered there, the power of an elaborate ceremonial and carefully preserved customs. Let us add to this revelation of literature a personal acquaintance with a young man whose affection and loyalty, whose tenderest human ties and domestic training are pulling one way against the taste and desires of a personality which constantly draws him into pursuits and interests outside of the family life. We may see, day after day, his attempts to attend ceremonies for which he no longer cares, his efforts to interest his father in other questions, and to transfer his religious zeal to social problems. We have added to Zangwill's art by our personal acquaintance, a dramatic force which even he could not portray. We may easily know a daughter who might earn much more money as a stenographer, could she work from Monday morning to Saturday night, but who quietly and docilely makes neckties for low wages because she can thus abstain from work Saturdays, to please her father. She goes without the clothes she otherwise might have, she identifies herself with girls whom she does not care for, in order to avoid the break which would be so desperate. Without Zangwill's illumination we would have to accumulate much more experience, but it is no compliment to the artist, if, having read him, we feel no desire for experience itself.

After all, the only world we know is that of Appreciation, but we grow more and more discontented with a mere intellectual apprehension, and wish to move forward from a limited and therefore obscure understanding of life to a larger and more embracing one, not only with our minds, but with all our powers of life. Our craving for art is a desire to appreciate emotionally, our craving for life is a desire to move forward organically.

I know little Italian boys who joyfully drop their English the moment they are outside the school-room door; and others of them who are teaching the entire family and forming a connection between them and the outside world, interpreting political speeches and newspapers and eagerly transforming Italian customs into American ones. One watches the individual boy with great interest, to see whether he will faithfully make himself a transmitter and helper, or whether he will be stupidly pleased with his achievements, and consider his examinations the aim of his life. I sometimes find myself nervously watching a young man or woman in a university in much the same way, and applying essentially the same test. I wonder whether his knowledge will in the end exercise supreme sway over him, so that he will come to consider it "a self-sufficing purveyor of reality," and care for nothing further, whether he will become, in the end, "school bound" with his faculties well trained for acquisition, but quite useless in other directions. To test a student's knowledge of Italian history by a series of examinations is possible; to test his genuine interest in that great boot thrust into the Mediterranean is to know whether or not he conquers a comparatively easy language, whether he traces in the large Italian colony of his city the hero-worship and higher aims evoked by Garibaldi as they are gradually seized upon by the ward politician and converted to ignoble ends; whether he feels a certain shame that, although Mazzini dedicated to the working men of Italy his highest ethical and philosophical appeal so that a desire for a republic had much to do with their coming to America, no great teacher of either ethics or politics has ever devoted himself to the Italians in America. Just as we do not know a fact until we can play with it, so we do not possess knowledge until we have an impulse to bring it into use; not the didactic impulse, not the propagandist impulse, but that which would throw into the stream of common human experience one bit of important or historic knowledge, however small, which before belonged to a few.

The phrase "applied knowledge" or science has so long been used in connection with polytechnic schools that it may be well to explain that I am using it in a broader sense. These schools have applied science primarily for professional ends. They are not so commercial, but they may easily become quite as specialized in their departments as the chemical laboratories attached to certain large manufacturing concerns. In the early days of Johns Hopkins University, one of the men in the biological department invented a contrivance which produced a very great improvement in the oyster raft at that time in use in the Chesapeake Bay. For months afterward, in all the commencement orations and other occasions when "prominent citizens" were invited to speak, this oyster raft was held up as the great contribution of the University to the commercial interest of the city, and as a justification of the University's existence, much to the mortification of the poor inventor. This, also, is an excellent example of what I do not mean.

The application which I have in mind is one which cannot be measured by its money-making value. I have in mind an application to a given neighborhood of the solace of literature, of the uplift of the imagination, and of the historic consciousness which gives its possessor a sense of connection with the men of the past who have thought and acted, an application of the stern mandates of science, not only to the conditions of sewers and the care of alleys, but to the methods of life and thought; the application of the metaphysic not only to the speculations of the philosopher, but to the events of the passing moment; the application of the moral code to the material life, the transforming of the economic relation into an ethical relation until the sense that religion itself embraces all relations, including the ungodly industrial relation, has become common property.

An ideal settlement would have no more regard for the "commercial" than would the most scientific of German seminars. The word application must be taken quite aside from its commercial or professional sense.

In this business of application, however, a settlement finds itself tending not only to make common those good things which before were partial and remote, but it finds itself challenging and testing by standards of moral democracy those things which it before regarded as good, if they could but be universal, and it sometimes finds that the so-called good things will not endure this test of being universalized. This may be illustrated by various good things. We may take first the so-called fine arts.

Let us consider the experience of a resident of a settlement who cares a great deal for that aspect and history of life, which has been portrayed in the fine arts. For years she has had classes studying through photographs and lectures the marbles of Greece, the paintings, the renaissance of Italy and the Gothic architecture of mediaeval Europe. She has brought into the lives of scores of people a quality of enjoyment, a revelation of experience which they never knew before. Some of them buy photographs to hang in their own houses, a public school art society is started, schoolroom walls are tinted and hung with copies of the best masters; so that in the end hundreds of people have grown familiar with the names of artists, and with conceptions of life which were hidden from them before. Some of these young women were they students of a fresh-water college could successfully pass an examination in the "History of Art." The studio of Hull House is well filled with young men and women who successfully copy casts and paint accurately what they see around them, and several of them have been admitted to the Chicago Art Institute upon competitive scholarships. Now, the first of these achievements would certainly satisfy the average college teacher whose business it is faithfully to transmit the accumulations of knowledge upon a given subject, and, of course, if possible, to add to the sum total of that knowledge in the matter of arrangement or discovery. The second achievement would certainly satisfy the ordinary philanthropic intent, which is to give to others the good which it possesses. But a settlement would have little vitality if it were satisfied with either of these achievements, and would at once limit its scope to that of the school on the one hand, or that of philanthropy on the other. And a settlement is neither a school nor a philanthropy, nor yet a philanthropic school or a scholarly philanthropy.

A settlement looks about among its neighbors and finds a complete absence of art. It sees people working laboriously without that natural solace of labor which art gives; they have no opportunity of expressing their own thoughts to their fellows by means of that labor.

It finds the ambitious members of the neighborhood over-anxious and hurried. Wrapping up bars of soap in pieces of paper might at least give the pleasure of accuracy and repetition if it could be done at leisure but, when paid for by the piece, speed is the sole requirement, and the last suggestion of human interest has been taken away. The settlement soon discovers how impossible it is to put a fringe of art on the end of a day thus spent. It is not only bad pedagogics, but it is an impossible undertaking, to appeal to a sense of beauty and order which has been crushed by years of ugly and disorderly work. May I relate an experience of a friend of Hull House, who took a party of visitors to the Art Institute of Chicago? In a prominent place upon that excellent building there have been carved in good stone, and with some degree of skill, several fine, large skulls of oxen. The bulk of the settlement party had no armor of erudition with which to protect themselves against such hideousness, and the leader of the party carefully explained that in Greece, after a sacrifice was made, skulls of the animals were hung upon the temples. But when he came to tell why they were upon the Art Institute of Chicago, he found his discourse going lame. That they were once religious symbols charged with meaning, was hardly a sufficient defence. They struck no response, certainly gave no delight nor sense of infection to the bewildered group who stood in front of them. It may be well to say in passing that this group were too unsophisticated to take great pride in the mere fact that they knew what this meant, as a club in search of culture would certainly have done. In his chagrin the Hull House friend found himself reflecting that the sacrifices, after all, did represent brotherhood and he made an attempt to compare them with the present symbols of brotherhood which are found upon the engraved charters hanging upon those walls which shelter the meetings of labor organizations. These charters make a sincere attempt to express the conviction of brotherhood, yet they have but the crudest symbolic representation, two hands clasping each other. It is not only that the print is cheap, but the hands are badly drawn and badly modeled; they express no tenderness nor firmness, and are done without any interpretive skill. The hands upon the old-fashioned tombstones which indicated a ghostly farewell might be interchanged with this pair of hands which indicate vital standing together, and no one would detect the difference. It occurred to this Hull House friend, with a sense of shame and chagrin, that the artists of Chicago had been recreant to their trust, that they had been so caught by a spirit of imitation that they slavishly represented the symbols of animal sacrifice which no longer existed, and kept away from a great human movement, which in America at least, has not yet found artistic expression. If the skulls had been merely an obsolete symbol of the brotherhood which had survived and developed its own artistic symbols, they might easily have been made intelligible and full of meaning. The experience of the resident who teaches the history of art, of the good friend who is ashamed of the lack of democracy and interpretive power among modern artists, added to many other bits of experience and emotion has resulted in the establishment of a Chicago Arts and Crafts Society, which was founded at Hull House more than a year ago. This society has developed an amazing vitality of its own. And perhaps a quotation from its constitution will show its trend:

"To consider the present state of the factories and the workmen therein, and to devise lines of development which shall retain the machine in so far as it relieves the workmen from drudgery, and tends to perfect his product but which shall insist that the machine be no longer allowed to dominate the workman and reduce his production into a mechanical distortion."

The Chicago Arts and Crafts Society has challenged the present condition and motive of art. Its protest is certainly feeble and may be ineffective, but it is at least genuine and vital. Under the direction of several of its enthusiastic members a shop has been opened at Hull House where articles are designed and made. It is not merely a school where people are taught and then sent forth to use their teaching in art according to their individual initiative and opportunity, but where those who have been carefully trained and taught may remain, to express the best they may in wood or metal. A settlement would avoid the always getting ready for life which seems to dog the school, and would begin with however small a group to really accomplish and to live.¹

This may indeed bring us quite naturally to the attitude of the settlement toward the organized education with which it is brought in contact, the two forms of organization being naturally the public school and university extension lectures.

The resident finds the use of the public school constantly limited because it occupies such an isolated place in the community. The school board and the teachers have insensibly assumed that they have to do exclusively with children, or a few adult evening classes, only in certain settled directions. The newly arrived South Italian peasants who come to the night schools are thoroughly ill-adjusted to all their surroundings. To change suddenly from picking olives to sewer extension is certainly a bewildering experience. They have not yet obtained control of their powers for the performance of even the humblest social service, and have no chance to realize within themselves the social relation of that service which they are performing. Feeling this vaguely perhaps, but very strongly as only a dull peasant mind can feel, they go to the night schools in search of education. They are taught to read and write concerning small natural objects, on the assumption that the undeveloped intellect works best with insects and tiny animals, and they patiently accept this uninteresting information because they expect "education" to be dull and hard. Never for an instant are their own problems of living in the midst of unfamiliar surroundings even touched upon. There seems to be a belief among educators that it is not possible for the mass of mankind to have experiences which are of themselves worth anything, and that accordingly, if a neighborhood is to receive valuable ideas at all, they must be brought in from the outside, and almost exclusively in the form of books. Such scepticism regarding the possibilities of human nature as has often been pointed out results in equipping even the youngest children with the tools of reading and writing, but gives them no real participation in the industrial and social life with which they come in contact.

The residents in a settlement know that for most of their small neighbors life will be spent in handling material things either in manufacturing or commercial processes, and yet little is done to unfold the fascinating history of industrial evolution or to illuminate for them the materials among which they will live. The settlement sees boys constantly leave school to enter the factory at fourteen or fifteen without either of the requirements involved in a social life, on the one hand "without a sense of the resources already accumulated," and on the other "without the individual ability to respond to those resources."

If it is one function of a settlement to hold a clue as to what to select and what to eliminate in the business of living, it would bring the same charge of overwrought detail against the university extension lectures. A course of lectures in astronomy, illustrated by "stereopticon slides," will attract a large audience the first week who hope to hear of the wonders of the heavens, and the relation of our earth thereto, but instead of that they are treated to spectrum analyses of star dust, or the latest theories concerning the milky way. The habit of research and the desire to say the latest word upon any subject overcoming any sympathetic understanding of his audience which the lecturer might otherwise develop.

The teachers in the night schools near Hull House struggle with Greeks and Armenians, with Bohemians and Italians, and many another nationality. I once suggested to a professor of anthropology in a neighboring university that he deliver a lecture to these bewildered teachers upon simple race characteristics and, if possible, give them some interest in their pupils, and some other attitude than that all persons who do not speak English are ignorant. The professor kindly consented to do this, but when the time came frankly acknowledged that he could not do it—that he had no information available for such a talk. I was disappointed, of course, and a little chagrined when, during the winter, three of his pupils came to me at different times, anxiously inquiring if I could not put them on the track of people who had six toes, or whose relatives had been possessed of six toes. It was inevitable that the old charge should occur to me, that the best trained scientists are inclined to give themselves over to an idle thirst for knowledge which lacks any relation to human life, and leave to the charlatans the task of teaching those things which deeply concern the welfare of mankind.

Tolstoy points out that the mass of men get their intellectual food from the abortive outcasts of science, who provide millions of books, pictures and shows, not to instruct and guide, but for the sake of their own profit and gain, while the real student too often stays in a laboratory, occupied in a mysterious activity called science. He does not even know what is required by the workingmen. He has quite forgotten their mode of life, their views of things and their language. Tolstoy claims that the student has lost sight of the fact that it is his duty, not to study and depict, but to serve. This is asking a great deal from one man, or even from one institution. It may be necessary that the university be supplemented by the settlement, or something answering thereto; but let the settlement people recognize the value of their own calling, and see to it that the university does not swallow the settlement, and turn it into one more laboratory: another place in which to analyze and depict, to observe and record. A settlement which performs but this function is merely an imitative and unendowed university, as a settlement which gives all its energies to classes and lectures and athletics is merely an imitative college. We ourselves may have given over attending classes and may be bored by lectures, but to still insist that working people shall have them is to take the priggish attitude we sometimes allow ourselves toward children, when we hold up rigid moral standards to them, although permitting ourselves a greater latitude. If without really testing the value of mental pabulum, we may assume it is nutritious and good for working people, because some one once assumed that it was good for us, we throw away the prerogative of a settlement, and fall into the rigidity of the conventional teacher.

The most popular lectures we ever had at Hull House were a series of twelve upon organic evolution, but we caught the man when he was but a university instructor, and his mind was still eager over the marvel of it all. Encouraged by this success we followed the course with other lectures in science, only to find our audience annihilated by men who spoke with dryness of manner and with the same terminology which they used in the class room.

A settlement might bring the same charge against university extension as against the public schools, that it is bookish and remote. Simple people want the large and vital—they are still in the tribal stage of knowledge, so to speak. It is not that simple people like to hear about little things; they want to hear about great things, simply told. We remember that the early nomads did not study the blades of grass at their feet, but the stars above their heads—although commercially considered, the study of grass would have been much more profitable.

These experiences would seem to testify that there is too much analysis in our thought, as there is too much anarchy in our action. Perhaps no one is following up this clue so energetically as Professor

Patrick Geddes in Edinburgh, who is attempting, not only to graphically visualize a synthesis, an encyclopedia of orderly knowledge, but in his own words—is endeavoring "to outline a correspondingly detailed synergy of orderly actions." The "regional survey" of knowledge which he takes from his outlook tower would thus pass into "regional activity."

So far as my experience goes a settlement finds itself curiously more companionable with the state and national bureaus in their efforts in collecting information and analyzing the situation, than it does with university efforts. This may possibly be traced to the fact that the data is accumulated by the bureaus on the assumption that it will finally become the basis for legislation, and is thus in the line of applicability. The settlements from the first have done more or less work under the direction of the bureaus. The head of a federal department quite recently begged a settlement to transform into readable matter a certain mass of material which had been carefully collected into tables and statistics. He hoped to make a connection between the information concerning diet and sanitary conditions, and the tenement house people who sadly needed this information. The head of the bureau said quite simply that he hoped that the settlements could accomplish this, not realizing that to put information into readable form is not nearly enough. It is to confuse a simple statement of knowledge with its application.

Permit me to illustrate from a group of Italian women who bring their underdeveloped children several times a week to Hull House for sanitary treatment, under the direction of a physician. It has been possible to teach some of these women to feed their children oatmeal instead of tea-soaked bread, but it has been done, not by statement at all but by a series of gay little Sunday morning breakfasts given to a group of them in the Hull House nursery. A nutritious diet was thus substituted for an inferior one by a social method. At the same time it was found that certain of the women hung bags of salt about their children's necks, to keep off the evil eye, which was supposed to give the children crooked legs at first, and in the end to cause them to waste away. The salt bags gradually disappeared under the influence of baths and cod liver oil. In short, rachitis was skillfully arrested, and without mention that disease was caused not by evil eye but by lack of cleanliness and nutrition, and without passing through the intermediate belief that disease was sent by Providence, the women form a little centre for the intelligent care of children, which is making itself felt in the Italian colony. Knowledge was applied in both cases, but scarcely as the statistician would have applied it.

We recall that the first colleges of the Anglo-Saxon race were established to educate religious teachers. For a long time it was considered the mission of the educated to prepare the mass of the people for the life beyond the grave. Knowledge dealt largely in theology, but it was ultimately to be applied, and the test of the successful graduate, after all, was not his learning, but his power to save souls. As the college changed from teaching theology to teaching secular knowledge the test of its success should have shifted from the power to save men's souls to the power to adjust them in healthful relations to nature and their fellow men. But the college failed to do this, and made the test of its success the mere collecting and disseminating of knowledge, elevating the means into an end and falling in love with its own achievement. The application of secular knowledge need be no more commercial and so-called practical than was the minister's when he applied his theology to the delicate problems of the human soul. This attempt at application on the part of the settlements may be, in fact, an apprehension of the situation.

It would be a curious result if this word "applied science," which the scholar has always been afraid of, lest it lead him into commercial influences, should have in it the salt of saving power, to rescue scholarship from the function of accumulating and transmitting to the higher and freer one of directing human life.

Recognizing the full risk of making an absurd, and as yet totally unsubstantiated claim, I would still express the belief that the settlement has made a genuine contribution in this direction by its effort to apply knowledge to life, to express life itself in terms of life.

In line with this conception are the efforts the settlement makes to mitigate the harshness of industry by this legal enactment. The residents are actuated, not by a vague desire to do good which may distinguish the philanthropist, nor by that thirst for data and analysis of the situation which so often distinguishes the "sociologist," but by the more intimate and human desire that the working man, quite aside from the question of the unemployed or the minimum wage, shall have secured to him powers of life and enjoyment, after he has painstakingly earned his subsistence; that he shall have an opportunity to develop those higher moral and intellectual qualities upon which depend the free aspects and values of living. Thus a settlement finds itself more and more working toward legal enactment, not only on behalf of working people, and not only in co-operation with them, but with every member of the community who is susceptible to the moral appeal. Labor legislation has always been difficult in America, largely owing to our optimism, and the comparative ease of passing from class to class. The sweater's victim, who hopes soon to be a contractor himself, will not take an interest in the law which may momentarily protect him but which may later operate against him. A man who is a bricklayer ambitious to become a master builder is not too eager that building regulations be made more stringent. In order to get a law, even to protect a small class of citizens, an appeal has to be made to the moral sense of the entire community, for one is barred from the very nature of the case from making a class appeal. Hundreds of girls are constantly impaired in health and vitality by long hours of factory work, yet each one of these girls is so confident of marrying out of her trade—each one regards her factory work as so provisional, that it is almost impossible to secure among them a concerted movement for improvement. To make a sensational appeal on their behalf or on behalf of the sweater's victims is undemocratic and often accentuates the consciousness of class difference. When the newspapers tell us of the horrors of the sweat shop, painting one shop with the various shades of blackness, found only in a dozen, until no human being however wretched could possibly work in such a shop, it becomes all the more difficult to set before the public mind what a reasonable workshop demands. Orderliness and cleanliness do not seem necessary to the mind sated with the horrors of contagious diseases. To impress upon such a mind that sweaters' employes live out but half the days of even the short life of the working man cannot arouse it to concern. When, in order to excite pity for one family a newspaper will degrade all humanity in the minds of the benevolent of the community, so that the statement that the poor lose fifty per cent of their children, does not seem startling if they die quietly in their beds and are not frozen and starved, is to increase the gulf beyond what actually exists. The sensational writer of short stories, who recklessly overstates and holds the exceptional as the habitual, does much to destroy the conception of human life, which experience has been slowly building up in the minds of the community. A reckless appeal to primitive pity may change conditions of a given case, but it sacrifices too much for the result.

A settlement in its attempt to apply the larger knowledge of life to industrial problems makes its appeal upon the assumption that the industrial problem is a social one, and the effort of a settlement in securing labor legislation is valuable largely in proportion as it can make both the working men and the rest of the community conscious of solidarity, and insists upon similarities rather than differences. A settlement constantly endeavors to make its neighborhood realize that it belongs to the city as a whole, and can only improve as the city improves. We, at Hull House, have undertaken to pave the streets of our ward only to find that we must agitate for an ordinance, that repaving shall be done from a general fund before we can hope to have our streets properly paved. We have attempted to compel by law, that the manufacturer provide proper work rooms for his sweater's victims, and were surprised to find ourselves holding a mass meeting in order to urge a federal measure upon Congress.

One of the residents at Hull House for three years faithfully inspected the alleys of our ward, but all her faithful service was set at naught because civil service has been but a farce in Chicago and to insist upon its administration, and the abolition of the contract system is the shortest method of cleaning the alleys.

The settlement was startled during October and November of last year by the occurrence of seven murders within a radius of ten blocks from Hull House, in a neighborhood of which we had always boasted that it was not criminal. A little investigation of details and motives, the accident of a personal acquaintance with two of the criminals, made it not in the least difficult to trace the murders back to the influence of the late war between Spain and the United States. The predatory instinct is not far back of most of us. Simple people who read of carnage and bloodshed easily receive a suggestion. Habits of self-control which have been but slowly and imperfectly acquired quickly break down. Some psychologists intimate that action germinates not only in the habitual thought, but may be traced to the selection of the subject upon which the attention is fixed and that it is by this decision of what shall hold the attention that the trend of action is determined. The newspapers, the posters, the street conversation for weeks had to do with war and threatening of war.

The little children in the street played at war day after day, although they did not play they were freeing Cubans, but on the contrary that they were killing Spaniards. For years the settlement had held that the life of each little child should be regarded as valuable, that the humane instinct should keep in abeyance any tendency to cruelty, that law and order should be observed, not only in letter, but in spirit, and it suddenly finds that a national event has thrown back all this effort.

There is no doubt that we grow more or less accustomed to faults and follies which we constantly see, and that a resident leaving one quarter of the city for another does get a fresher point of view. She comes in to an industrial neighborhood to find that the workingmen living there see those of their own numbers who have gradually yielded to a love of drink and have become drunkards, with a certain amount of indifference and leniency of judgment. Many of these wretched men have been kindly good natured fellows, and possessed of weak wills rather than vicious ones. The resident is shocked by this leniency, but in course of time she finds herself viewing business circles from a new point of view. A business man constantly sees men around him who have gradually yielded to a love of money until many of them have become perjurers, in order to avoid the payment of full taxes; some of them have lent themselves to debauching city councils and state legislatures in order to protect vested interests by "necessary legislation;" yet a business man finds himself tending to judge such conduct leniently because it is a temptation which he can understand, one to which he himself has more or less yielded at least by connivance, if not by participation. To habitually drink too much alcohol and neglect one's wife and children, or to annually perjure one's soul and neglect one's duty to the state, are not really so unlike in motive and consequence, to anyone who looks at them freely and from an equidistant standpoint.

Our attention has so long been called to the sins of the appetite and to the neglect of family obligations, that we fail to see these other equally great sins of cupidity and failure to respond to the social duty. To fail to see social dereliction in one class and point out moral failure in the drunkard shows a singular lack of understanding of the ethical problems which are now pressing upon us. Books have been written on the poverty and wretchedness which are the result of alcoholism, and it has indeed been overworked rather than underworked as a cause of social deterioration. Social disorders arising from conscienceless citizenship have yet to be made clear.

There are doubtless two dangers to which the settlement is easily susceptible. The first is the danger that it shall approach too nearly the spirit of the mission which, as Canon Barnett has recently pointed out, in the *Nineteenth Century Review*, will always exist, will always be needed, but which from its very nature can not be a settlement. Those who join it believe in some doctrines or methods which they wish to extend, it may be those of church, of socialists, of teetotalers, of political party; but followers are enlisted and organized and a vast amount of machinery created for a given aim. They will always be able to tell how many they have "reached, " and how many believe as they do. As Canon Barnett says there are moments when definiteness of doctrine and the measuring of men's motives must seem the most essential thing and at such times the settlement must appear ineffective; but so far as a settlement group is committed to one philosophy which it cares for above the meanings which life may teach, so far as definiteness precludes perception, so far as their minds are not free to rise and fall with their neighbor's minds, which are occupied with hundreds of cares and hopes, so far a settlement has failed.

The second danger is the tendency to lay stress upon what we might call "geographical salvation." All over the world from Russia west to Japan people are moving from country to town, with the conviction that they are finding more fullness of life. An advance guard may be said to be moving back from the town to the country, from the sprinkling of the very rich to the little colonies, found in England and America, who are protesting against the industrial system by getting out of it so far as possible. But within the limits of the city itself, also can be found this belief in geographical salvation. When a given neighborhood becomes shabby, or filled with foreigners, whose habits are unlike those of their neighbors, the best people in the neighborhood begin to move out, taking with them their initiative and natural leadership, as their parents had previously taken it from their native villages. A settlement deliberately selects such a neighborhood, and moves into it, but must not lay too much stress upon that fact in and of itself. Its social relations are successful as it touches to life the dreary and isolated, and brings them into a fuller participation of the common inheritance. Its teaching is successful as it makes easy and available that which was difficult and remote. Its most valuable function as yet, lies along the line of interpretation and synthesis.

JANE ADDAMS.

Hull House, Chicago

A FUNCTION OF THE SOCIAL SETTLEMENT

[1] All of us who have been through the old-fashioned school and college can remember the tedium and confusion of always getting ready for something, of preparing for the life which was to follow school. We may remember how it affected our moral natures as well. We were in a hurry now, but we would be more leisurely and kindly when we finished school. We came to have a firm belief that a new and strong moral nature would be given to us at the time we received our diplomas; and this attitude of preparation is easily carried over into life beyond the school.